Brooke Young Sparks

Brown Brené. The Gifts of Imperfection: Let Go of Who You Think You're Supposed to Be and Embrace Who You Are. Instaread Summaries, 2014.

Card, Michael. Scribbling in the Sand: Christ and Creativity. InterVarsity Press, 2004.
Holy Bible: New International Version. Zondervan, 2005.

Schaeffer, Francis A. Art and the Bible. InterVarsity Press, 2009.

TerKeurst, Lysa. Unglued Devotional: 60 Days of Imperfect Progress. Zondervan, 2012.

Warren, Tish Harrison. Liturgy of the Ordinary - Sacred Practices in Everyday Life. Intervarsity

Welcome

IN THE PURSUIT of the ever elusive peaceful life I so desire, I'm finding that instead of eliminating certain things in my daily life, it has been more advantageous to cultivate creativity, choose joy, practice gratitude, and seek stillness and solitude in order to experience true peace that only comes from God. My hope is that over the next several weeks, diving into God's Word and exploring the scriptures, we will begin to see who we are created to be and how through implementing simple practices we invite God into the sacred space we currently inhabit.

In these next four weeks may Peace Like a River flow from His Word, through the work of the Holy Spirit bringing about the only peace that surpasses our earthly understanding. My prayer is that the abundance of the Holy Spirit would stream steadily through these pages from His Word to your heart and into your daily life.

Peace be with you, my friend

CULTIVATE *Creativity*
WEEK 1

> "Open your eyes to the beauty that is unveiled through the Scriptures and the gospel of Jesus Christ. Come alive to the freedom that is uniquely yours to create to the glory of God."
>
> MICHAEL CARD
> Scribbling in the Sand

Through my quest for peace, I'm learning that "In the beginning God created" is a personal message and mandate for me as it is for the world. God is our Creator and according to Genesis 1:26, "They (Father, Son, and Holy Spirit) made us in their image". We are image bearers of the Creator God. We were made to create! We are like God, but not divine.

Three words I never heard growing up were, "You are creative." I grew up with a narrative that implied I was not creative. I didn't do anything beautiful exceptionally well. My definition of creativity was doing something that is both beautiful and exceptional. I was a scrawny, freckle-faced, curly-haired, white-legged little girl who thought she had nothing of exceptional value to offer anyone. I was not a stand-out in any academic area, nor did I sing, play an instrument, draw anything other than a stick figure and a sunshine. I loved dance and felt that watching the lyrical dancers would translate into my body moving with the same style and grace, but that did not happen. I lacked the coordination and technique that was usually required to move up from the back row. The overarching message was, you are average, at best.

My mother exuded creativity. She painted flowers and nature scenes before I was born. She learned to sew from her grandmother and made all of the Holly Hobby baby bedding for my room, so I was told. She taught herself how to play the guitar and sang and wrote songs. However, because of her debilitating mental illness, she was too sick to pass on any of those creative expressions to her daughter. As a young adult, I struggled to think creatively. I've probably spoken the words "I'm not creative" over a million times. Until now. I'm not going to allow those three words to come out of my mouth again. What I've been learning is that we are ALL created creative. According to Dr. Brene' Brown, we either cultivate it, stuff it, or it hides until we finally discover it. May we not wait one more day. May we believe that what the God of the universe says about each of us and may we walk in His truth. You were made to be creative and creativity helps us experience peace.

"Do we understand the freedom we have under the lordship of Christ and the norms of Scripture? Is the creative part of our life committed to Christ? Christ is the Lord of our whole life and the Christian life should produce not only truth - flaming truth - but also beauty."

FRANCIS A. SCHAEFFER

Art and the Bible (p. 48)

cultivate creativity

DAY 1

Read

Genesis 1:26-27

Focus

In these verses identify the concept of the wholeness of man and lordship of man over creation.

Cultivate Creativity

Who were the ones who bore the image of God?

What were they to be in charge of?

What were they to do with it before the Lord?

DAY 2

cultivate creativity

Read

Galatians 6:4-5

Focus

The NIV encourages us to "carry our own load" but I love how The Message (if you don't have a copy, it's printed for you under "Sunday Reflection") urges us to do our "creative best" with what God has uniquely given us.

Cultivate Creativity

What is your "creative best"?

Have you ever thought about how you are uniquely designed to create?

In what areas do your creative juices flow in your life, past or present?

How can those be cultivated to the glory of God?

cultivate creativity

DAY 3

Read

Read Exodus 31:1-11

Focus

In this section of scripture, God has chosen Bezalel and given him wisdom, understanding, and skills to do the work He had chosen for him to do.

Cultivate Creativity

List the skills specifically needed for the jobs the Lord had ordained for Bezalel and his helper to complete. Do any of the skills or craftsmanship stand out to you as an area in which you have been uniquely gifted. An interior designer friend and and a friend who makes wooden decorative pieces for homes immediately comes to my mind. Thank God for your unique gifting.

DAY 4

cultivate creativity

Read

Exodus 35:35

Focus

List the skills, jobs, and colors necessary in this verse.

Cultivate Creativity

What are some ways that you experience pleasure, delight, beauty, and artistry? How has God uniquely equipped you to reflect His creativity? This week, plan a specific time or way to get your creative juices flowing. Consider taking a trip to a museum or garden, write a poem or song of praise or thanksgiving, paint a small canvas, plan an activity for your family-however you feel inspired through an act of creativity.

cultivate creativity

DAY 5

Read

Isaiah 43:18-19

Focus

What "new thing" has He recently begun to do within you?

Cultivate Creativity

Make a T-chart. On the left side write 3-5 discouraging messages you tell yourself that keep you stuck. On the right side describe 3-5 ways God has creatively gifted you to glorify Him uniquely. Use different colors or symbols if that gets your mind motivated.

DAY 6

cultivate creativity

Read

Colossians 3:23

Focus

Who should we be seeking to glorify with our work, creative or mundane?

Cultivate Creativity

How can you make something you already do an act of worship to God?

**cultivate
creativity**

DAY 7

Sunday Reflection

"Make a careful exploration of who you are and the work you have been given, and then sink yourself into that. Don't be impressed with yourself. Don't compare yourself with others. Each of you must take responsibility for doing the creative best you can with your own life."

GALATIANS 6:4-5

The Message

CHOOSE *Joy*
WEEK 2

I just don't have it today. I'm not motivated to
work on my work. I've carpooled kids to school,
taken one to the dentist, two for haircuts,
homeschooled another, rocked and read to
the littlest one and put her down for a nap.
I'm spent for the day, it's only 12:38 pm. I feel
anxious, fretful, and immobile for anything
worthy of the Lord. What can I do now?

I can choose one of the gifts of imperfection.
I can take a nap with my little one and not
feel bad about it one bit, or I can say a prayer,
light a candle, make a cup of peppermint tea
or listen to Chris Rice sing beloved Hymns
on my back porch. I can write, read, study, sit
outside, take a walk or create something. I have
a choice to choose joy today. Joy is ultimately
from God, and He wants me to have it because
it's through His joy that shines through me
that those around me are drawn to Him.

choose joy

Sometimes I feel as though our culture has given us a license to sin. We are encouraged to grumble and complain about our daily activities which squelches our ability to see blessing in the mundane. When we focus on our selfishness we trade peace for anxiety. When we choose joy we are in essence pursuing peace.

Read

Romans 15:13

Focus

How does a believer become filled with joy and peace? Where does the believer's power come from? What is our hope in?

Choose Joy

Joy and peace can be found in mundane tasks that we prioritize every day. How can you make something you do every day a peaceful or joy filled practice? For example, with a family of six, I do a lot of laundry! It's easy to despise this mundane task. I love listening to books on Audible or podcasts. I now use my "laundry time" to listen. This has turned a drudgery into a diversion that produces joy. Think of an example like this that pertains to your daily life.

DAY 9

choose joy

Read

Isaiah 55:12-13

Focus

In Isaiah chapter 55 we see an invitation from the Savior to receive freely the blessings of joy and peace. His fullness is evident in the natural world He created. The Lord is gracious to all. It is not in vain that we seek to follow the Holy Spirit's guidance. We are free to look into the fullness of His wonderful grace. How will we go out? What will we be led by? List the plants in verse 13 that will become a memorial to the Lord.

Choose Joy

Think about peaceful scenes that God has created in nature for your pleasure. Make a list of colors and places in nature that bring to mind peace and joy. Take a walk, ride a bike, take a car ride, take time in the backyard or local park observing your own natural surroundings. Afterwards write down 5 observations from your time outside that bring to mind peace and joy.

choose joy

DAY 10

Read

Revelation 2:2-5

Focus

In your bible underline the 2nd half of verse 5: "Do the things you did at first."

If you are anything like me, you start out with a bang and begin to fizzle out about two-three weeks into your "new thing". It's about time, right? We're into our second week with three and a half to go and you're feeling tired, overwhelmed, dry. If you're not, let me just confess that I am! I heard a DJ on a Christian morning radio show point out this verse about doing the "deeds you did at first (NASB)". Like when you just aren't feelin' it...do what you know to do. This could pertain to our marriages when we're in a rut or parenting when you feel like you're doing laundry for people that live in your house that you haven't even met! Or it could be in your walk with the Lord. It's a journey, not a sprint, and when you feel like you're living in the trenches with toddlers or teenagers, or in my case both/and, the days can get long. Remembering the basics has the power to calm the chaos inside and out.

Choose Joy

Take time to remember the "deeds you did at first".
What do you know to do when the days get long?
Write it down. Ask God to help you do the next thing.

DAY 11

choose joy

Read

Psalm 94:19

Focus

How can you position yourself today to experience God? For me, it is purposely getting still and quiet. With four children that can be a challenge in my house. Last night was particularly chaotic during dinnertime. We all sat at the table going through our highs and lows for the day when one child decided he was "just too cool" for family dinner and got up and walked off. That required a parenting intervention from both my husband and me. Dinner stopped and redirection and restoration had to begin. After all was said and done and everyone had eaten, I looked around at the kitchen and started to wilt from my overwhelming thoughts. I knew that digging into the work-load was not going to give me perspective or peace. I left all as it was and went to go take a bath - not my usual modus operandi at this time of evening. I wasn't in there long, but it did give me a chance to breathe, pray, and receive from the Lord. When I emerged, I had a renewed sense of refreshment to reevaluate what needed to be done.

Choose Joy

Remind yourself of 3-5 "go-to's" that help you gain perspective and receive joy and peace during periods of chaos or confusion.

choose joy

DAY 12

Read

Job 33:26

Focus

What is joy the result of in this passage? You can experience true joy after repenting of sin with a contrite heart. The Lord looks at us through the righteousness of Christ. Many times our prayer life looks like a Christmas list asking for blessings and gifts from God to ourselves and those we love. There is a restorative joy that follows true confession. As believers we are to face our sin with sorrow at how we have dishonored God with our words and actions. When we do this, He is faithful and just to forgive us, cleanse us (1 John 1:9) and restore the joy of our salvation (Psalm 51:12). Ask God to reveal any unconfessed sin to you and practice repentance.

Choose Joy

Do you practice regular repentance to the Lord? What does this time look like for you?

DAY 13

choose joy

Read

Psalm 51:12

Focus

After the believer has been comforted in his affliction of sin, he or she desires restoration and renewal to holiness as much as joy of salvation. Barnes' commentary explains that "Restore unto me the joy of my salvation" literally means "Cause the joy of my salvation to return." This implies that he or she had known the true joy of being a friend of God, and of having a hope that was not dependant upon the circumstances of the day. That joy had been taken from him or her by his or her sin, yet restored by our gracious God.

Choose Joy

Explain in your own words how you came to faith in Christ and take time to remember the joy of that experience. A conversion experience could be at a specific time and place or event but could also be a season of change, a continual "working out" (Philippians 2:12) over time.

choose joy

DAY 14

Sunday Reflection

"Therefore, my dear friends, as you have always obeyed—not only in my presence, but now much more in my absence—continue to work out your salvation with fear and trembling, for it is God who works in you to will and to act in order to fulfill His good purpose."

PHILIPPIANS 2:12-13

PRACTICE *Gratitude*
WEEK 3

Research from Professor Brene' Brown's study on the subject of shame found that gratitude and joy are interconnected. You can't have one without the other. It makes sense really. A grateful person has much to be joyous about and vice versa. She also notes that there is nothing effective about having simply "an attitude of gratitude" but that gratitude, to be effective and sustaining, must be practiced. This is good news for those of us who may not always wake up on the bright side and for those of us who grew up with an unreliable narrative in our homes. We can actually begin the practices of gratitude and become grateful, joyful people who love God and love others.

So, that leaves me to ask, what do grateful people do? According to Dr. Brown's research they:

1) Write down what they are grateful for.

2) Pray daily prayers of gratitude.

3) Create gratitude expressions of art.

4) Pause during the busyness and stress of the day to say aloud "I am grateful for. . .".

practice gratitude

DAY 15

Read

1 Thessalonians 5:16-24

Focus

What is God's will for your life in Christ Jesus?

Practice Gratitude

This passage of scripture calls God "the God of peace" who "sanctifies you through and through". How can rejecting joy, prayer, and thankfulness "quench the Spirit" within you?

DAY 16

practice gratitude

Read

1 Timothy 4:15

Focus

What things will you put into practice? In what areas will you immerse yourself? How will you measure your imperfect progress?

Practice Gratitude

Begin with the 1st gratitude practice of writing down what you're thankful for. Challenge yourself to write down one thing you are thankful for each day for 1 month, during a season, or for 1 year. Gary Thomas, author of Sacred Marriage challenges husbands and wives to write down one thing everyday of the year that you are thankful for specifically pertaining to your spouse. Each day must be different. When you are done you will have 365 gratitude reflections. I'm challenging myself to do this. Will you?

practice gratitude

DAY 17

Read

Matthew 5:9

Focus

Think of ways you can bring peace into challenging relationships or feelings of anxiety with your friends or family.

Practice Gratitude

Write a letter of gratitude thanking someone whom you may consider an "enemy" or challenging relationship for the blessing they've brought to your life or write a prayer to God thanking Him for the gifts that person has been to you or others. You may never send the letter or show anyone the prayer but expressing gratitude is an exercise that will begin transforming your mind from hating your enemies to becoming an agent of peace.

DAY 18

practice gratitude

Read

Philippians 4:8

Focus

Dissect this verse: What is one thing that is a truth from God? What is something that is a noble action? What is one thing that God calls right or righteous? Name something that is pure? What is lovely about this world God created? What is an admirable action? Name something that is excellent or praiseworthy from the Lord?

Practice Gratitude

Sometimes, on a hard day, it's challenging to think of something to be grateful for. Really contemplating this verse in Philippians lays out a helpful guide to what is worth thanking Him for. Do the second gratitude practice of grateful people and pray a prayer of gratitude to the Lord who is sovereign over all.

practice gratitude

DAY 19

Read

Romans 8:26

Focus

Maybe we need to just sit still today. If you are like me, there are days when I have no more words. I am so overwhelmed by the things that occupy my head and heart, whether it be the task at hand, the hurting child in my arms or the husband I love who feels a million miles away. Isn't it the most comforting thing to know that the Holy Spirit intercedes on our behalf? We can simply say "thank you" today and nothing more. When I experience those deep feelings of loss and anguish, sadness and sorrow I say "Holy Spirit, you know what I do not. Pray for me and through me in Jesus' name, Amen"

Practice Gratitude

Give yourself an opportunity to practice the third practice of grateful people. Create a tangible expression of gratitude.

DAY 20

practice gratitude

Read

Romans 6:12-13

Focus

What is an "instrument of righteousness"? In her book, Preaching That Speaks to Women, Alice P. Mathews explains that righteousness is not simply right living but also right relating. This understanding was eye-opening for me because how I relate to others is important to God. He wants me to offer my relationships to Him, not just my actions. Acknowledging this allows these relationships to come under His Lordship, to become pleasing in His sight and to be used for His glory.

Practice Gratitude

Put the fourth "best practice" of grateful people to work. Take time to say aloud "I am grateful for..." and list the first things that the Holy Spirit brings to mind.

practice gratitude

DAY 21

Sunday Reflection

Rejoice always, pray continually, give thanks in all circumstances; for this is God's will for you in Christ Jesus. Do not quench the Spirit. Do not treat prophecies with contempt but test them all; hold on to what is good, reject every kind of evil. May God himself, the God of peace, sanctify you through and through. May your whole spirit, soul and body be kept blameless at the coming of our Lord Jesus Christ. The One who calls you is faithful, and He will do it.

1 Thessalonians 5:16-24

SEEK
Stillness and Solitude

WEEK 4

I want God to meet me in the beautiful, silent place. I want to hear Him speak, yet when I think of hearing from the Almighty, I think of the sounds of crashing waves against the golden coast of California, the smell of salt in the air and warm sunshine on my freckled arms and legs. I don't think of hearing Him while I'm sitting on the floor between the bed and the wall in my room stealing three minutes of solitude before a child cries out "Mama". However, that's exactly where He wants to speak to me, in the mundane ministry of my everyday. Hearing from God does not require a vacation, it only requires stillness.

We have a tendency to activity. Prayer and stillness is an offering. I present myself to the work of the Creator when I sit still and seek solitude just to listen, wait, and anticipate His presence in my daily life.

seek stillness and solitude

DAY 22

Read

Psalm 46:10

Focus

Contemplate who God is.

Seek Stillness and Solitude

"Be still" in this verse is not a gentle suggestion. It is a mandate to cease striving and stop. Plan for time each day to cease striving and be still before God to remember who He is.

DAY 23

seek stillness and solitude

I'm impatient. Productivity is my god. I need to learn the art of waiting. Waiting is a gift. It affords me time to consider the ways of God, the Creator of the Universe, the Author of life, the Good Father. James K.A. Smith says the incessantness of our culture must be resisted if we are to be a people set apart. He says "In the midst of our culture's tendency to embrace constant revelry that leaves us feeling hung-over and empty, we are people in training, together learning to wait."

Read

Psalm 119:15

Focus

Think about the passage of time, the hope for what we do not yet see. What are the ways of God that come to your mind?

Seek Stillness and Solitude

How can you practice the holy ways of waiting, hoping, slowing down, preparing your heart to receive and anticipate Christ in your life?

seek stillness and solitude
DAY 24

I live with the illusion that I am in control of the clock. I believe with my actions that I can become my own master. Time is not a commodity, but a gift. Time revolves around God, pointing to what He has done, what He is doing, and what He will do.

Read

Psalm 90:12

Focus

What does God want you to remember about Him and about yourself from this verse?

Seek Stillness and Solitude

In Luke 15:16 the Word tells us that Jesus withdrew in solitude to pray. How can you withdraw in solitude and pray as a practice adopted from Jesus.

DAY 25

seek stillness and solitude

God is at work in and through us as we wait. It is active and purposeful, not a waste of time. We are so conditioned to be productive that waiting is painful. But, if we look deeper, we begin to see the benefits outweigh the costs.

Read

Romans 8:25

Focus

What do we hope for? How are we oriented toward a future hope but created for our present reality? Are those opposing forces or are they complementary?

Seek Stillness and Solitude

Think about what you are striving to produce? How does it measure in the light of eternity? Are you spending your days toiling over futile idols of the "good life" or are you rooted in the reality of Christ's coming?

seek stillness and solitude
DAY 26

Rest or restlessness forms us over time. Sleep habits reveal our loves, idols of our culture. My willingness to resist sleep in order to pack in as much productivity as a 24 hour day can hold illuminates my desire to live as a machine instead of a creature with a Creator. Our Creator is the only one who does not sleep nor slumber. Sleep invites us to rely on Him, remember that we are finite. The holiness of rest and unproductivity is a gift from God.

Read

Psalm 4:8

Focus

Take an inventory of your sleep habits and the habits of those whose sleep habits affect you the most.

Seek Stillness and Solitude

A dear friend who is an interior designer and considered "creative" by anyone's standards reminded me that the acts of motherhood are innately creative. She suggested that it takes creativity to plan and implement activities for the betterment of our children and families. Utilize your God-given creativity and examine your household's evening activities. Are they conducive to healthy sleep patterns or do some things need to be added or subtracted from your schedules or habits to facilitate peace and tranquility at night? What are your family's activities saying about your beliefs about God?

DAY 27

seek stillness and solitude

Read

Exodus 20:8-11

Focus

Reflect on how the practice of a weekly day of rest affects you and your view of time, limits, your body, and God.

Seek Stillness and Solitude

If you do not practice a weekly day of rest, do so this week. Recognizing and celebrating the Sabbath is more than simply attending a weekend church service. Explore this biblical mandate and what it entails.

seek stillness and solitude

DAY 28

Sunday Reflection

"Remember the Sabbath day, to keep it holy. Six days you shall labor, and do all your work, but the seventh day is a Sabbath to the Lord your God. On it you shall not do any work, you, or your son, or your daughter, your male servant, or your female servant, or your livestock, or the sojourner who is within your gates. For in six days the Lord made heaven and earth, the sea, and all that is in them, and rested on the seventh day. Therefore the Lord blessed the Sabbath day and made it holy."

EXODUS 20:8-11

PURSUE Peace

WEEK 5

A quick internet search on peace will reveal a simplistic understanding of the word including free from disturbance or distraction, harmonious well-being, order, and lack of fear. Contrary to the world's point of view, the scriptures present the idea that peace is not connected to our outward circumstances. True peace is impossible to explain apart from an act of the Holy Spirit within the heart and mind of a believer.

pursue peace

DAY 29

Read

Matthew 3: 13-17

Focus

What has Jesus done to deserve his Father's adoration at this point? In the book, Liturgy of the ordinary, Tish Harrison Warren remarks that when the Father declares at Jesus' baptism, "This is my beloved Son, with whom I am well pleased, Jesus hasn't yet done much of anything that many would find impressive." At this point in the gospels, Jesus hasn't yet healed anyone, performed miracles, or resisted Satan, yet God announces His love and validation.

Pursue Peace

Do you see yourself as blessed and sent? Do you feel that you must earn the Father's approval and validation? In what ways do you strive to do this? Do you divide your secular work from your spiritual life?

DAY 30

pursue peace

Read

Psalm 34:14

Focus

Identify the the 4 action words in the passage and list them here.

Pursue Peace

Annie Dillard sums up the acts of daily work by saying "How we spend our days, is of course, how we spend our lives". How do you define "peace" in action? List 4 practices that ignite peace in your day.

pursue peace

DAY 31

Read

James 3:18

Focus

Define Peacemakers. List two things you personally are sowing into your life that will reap a harvest of righteousness.

Pursue Peace

Depict mundane activities whose regularity and steadfastness bring you calmness. Draw a scene or symbol, write a poem, or listen to a song and think about the words or melody that draws your heart to peacefulness.

DAY 32

pursue peace

Read

Proverbs 12:20

Focus

What do those who plan peace receive?

Pursue Peace

I don't know about you, but the winter weather can give me the blues. As a little girl I hated the cold, gloomy winter months. It seemed as though the world was moving a bit slower, there were less resources to go around in my home. For the last few years, I have made a decision to relish the winter as a time of rest and rejuvenation. I love the fresh start it brings and have fallen in love with the cool tones of gray, blue, and green. I started decorating my home in a special way during the winter months adding a few items like white candles, green pine branches, pine cones with blue winter berries as accents on my mantle and black and white patterned throw pillows on my couch. The simple added touches make me feel like my home is an inviting space and aesthetically pleasing. The bible is clear in the depictions of beauty that God bestows upon the earth and in the hearts of human beings. Think about the four seasons and write down which stand out as your favorites and why. Also, think about the one you dislike the most and jot down ideas to create a pleasing space during that time.

pursue peace

DAY 33

Read

Hebrews 12:14

Focus

How does one pursue peace? One commentary compares pursuing peace to the way a beast pursues his prey. He is listening for it, following it, and distracted by little around him. The beast finds traces of it and is diligent in his pursuit.

Pursue Peace

How do you actively pursue peace in your different vocations? For example, I am a mother, a wife, a storyteller, a friend and I pursue peace differently in all of those roles.

DAY 34

pursue peace

Read

Isaiah 9:6

Focus

Who is Jesus as described in Isaiah 9:6? What is he called? What is a truth that can always bring you peace?

Pursue Peace

Write out four areas or situations of anxiety, confusion, or fear in your life right now and next to them write one of each of the four attributes of Jesus described in the verse above.

pursue peace   **DAY 35**

Sunday Reflection

"And the peace of God, which surpasses all understanding, will guard your hearts and minds in Christ Jesus."

PHILIPPIANS 4:7

Reflection AND Transformation

WEEK 6

Let's reflect back on what God has taught us through His creation and through the steadfast regularity of our daily work. Invite Him to *Abide* in your specific ministry of the mundane.

"Abide in me, and I in you.
As the branch cannot
bear fruit by itself, unless
it abides in the vine,
neither can you,
unless you abide in me.

I am the vine; you are the branches.
Whoever abides in me and I in him
bears much fruit"

JOHN 15:4-5A

cultivate creativity

DAY 36

Isaiah 43:18-19

Do you believe you were made to be creative by the Creator? Are you doing your creative best?

Are you currently cultivating creativity, hiding it, or stuffing it? In what ways? Be specific in your self assessment.

What "new thing" has God begun to do in you? Take time to thank Him today.

 choose joy

Isaiah 55:12-13

In what specific ways are you actively "going out in joy" and "being lead forth in peace"?

Joy and peace can be found in mundane tasks. What daily tasks are you choosing to do with joy?

How are you choosing to position yourself each day to experience God?

practice gratitude

DAY 38

ead

1 Thessalonians 5:16-24

Look back at Week 3 and remember what you wrote down that you were thankful for?

Look at the four gratitude practices we learned from Dr. Brene' Brown and choose one activity and do it today.

DAY 39

seek stillness and solitude

ead

Psalm 46:10

Have you planned for time each day to "cease striving" and "be still" before God to remember who He is?

If you have not yet incorporated solitude into your day, start today. Sit in silence for 3 minutes. When finished, write your thoughts.

pursue peace

DAY 40

Psalm 34:14

Do you believe the idea that how you spend your day is how you spend your life? How do you spend your day. Write a time log for 1 typical day.

How many "mundane" activities are repeated day after day throughout a regular week? Thank God for the steadfast regularity this provides you and ask Him how you can bring Him into those activities in specific ways. Write down what the Holy Spirit reveals to you.

DAY 41

peace like a river

ead

Genesis 1:26

Do you believe that you were made in the image of God? What do you think that entails?

Which of the weeks spoke personally to you? How? How is God speaking to you about cultivating peace in your life going forward?

sunday reflection
DAY 42

Over the course of these six sacred weeks I hope you have been able to make connections with your daily practices as small, yet signifcant acts of worship to the Lord. Offer your work and creativity as a living sacrifice and invite God to be present and active.

IT IS WELL WITH MY SOUL

When peace like a river, attendeth my way,
When sorrows like sea billows roll
Whatever my lot, thou hast taught me to say
It is well, it is well, with my soul
It is well
With my soul
It is well, it is well with my soul

Though Satan should buffet, though trials should come,
Let this blest assurance control,
That Christ has regarded my helpless estate,
And hath shed His own blood for my soul
It is well (it is well)
With my soul (with my soul)
It is well, it is well with my soul

My sin, oh, the bliss of this glorious thought
My sin, not in part but the whole,
Is nailed to the cross, and I bear it no more,
Praise the Lord, praise the Lord, o my soul
It is well (it is well)
With my soul (with my soul)

It is well, it is well with my soul
It is well (it is well)
With my soul (with my soul)
It is well, it is well with my soul

HORATIO SPAFFORD 1876

Acknowledgements

There are so many sweet friends and content creators who have given of their time and talents to work on this project to the Glory of God and I'm so thankful.

Meredith Stanley is a beacon of grace and creativity and tirelessly worked to produce this work of art you hold in your hands. She continually brings beauty from ashes and spurs me on to continue pursuing the heart of God in my daily life. I'm so blessed to call her friend, neighbor and partner in ministry.

Lindsey Vannett, my bestie for the restie and librarian has been a trusted confidant for over 27 years. She took time away from work and family to edit content and grammar of this project, of which there were countless mistakes. She cheers me on in ministry and motherhood and I know we'll still be best friends in our 80's with blue hair laughing hysterically over upside down pizza.

Leigh Ann Yerrick is wise beyond her years and has become someone I admire for her walk with the Lord, love for her husband, and creativity with her children. She is the definition of grace under pressure. She edited content for comprehension and understanding and pointed out my blind spots, of which I have many, with love and truth. She draws me closer to the Lord with every interaction.

Rachael Johnson offers ideas and suggestions in the most relevant way. She was there at the inception of this project and continues to push me to press on toward the goal. She speaks the truth in love and allows me to be myself and loves me inspite of all my flaws. I'm so grateful for her insight and encouragement.

Austin, my husband, my friend, my partner in life and parenthood, I couldn't love you more. Hearing you say "I'm so proud of you" is the motivation that propels me forward in this ministry. I wouldn't want anyone else by my side. Thank you for your continued support of my dreams that result in zero financial return. Your steadfast regularity allows me to step out of my comfort zone and into faithful obedience.

Photo by Meredith Joyce at It's a Joyfyl Life Photography

Brooke Young Sparks, M.Ed., is a storyteller who traded the public school classroom for a laundry room/home office. She spends her days at home reading, writing and homeschooling. When she's not at home, Brooke can be found carpooling around town with her four kids, toddler to teen, in her "mom mobile" or in the classroom at Dallas Theological Seminary. She loves sharing hilarious stories of adventures with her family while skillfully weaving God's beautiful gift of redemption into every episode. She loves speaking to women about their daily lives, encouraging and equipping them with God's word. Her News Years resolutions included making her bed, taking daily walks in the sunshine and eating more cupcakes.

Photo by Lauren Clark of Lauren Clark Photography

Design and Layout: Meredith Stanley

Meredith Stanley, mother of three and designer by trade, enjoys passionately pursuing all artistic missions God throws her way. Armed with a degree in interior design and a lifetime of art education, she has sought to glorify God through commercial and residental interior design, church design, photography, illustration and graphic design. She truly considers each opportunity a blessing and loves seeing how God will use the talents He has given her to do great things. In her "spare time" she dreams of sipping coffee while listening to live acoustic music at a bustling downtown cat cafe, but in reality she changes diapers, watches far too many eposides of Octonauts and finds joy walking down the aisles of Aldi.

Made in the USA
Middletown, DE
25 March 2019